Delaney The Cat Burglar

DELANEY

THE CAT BURGLAR

by

PAMELA A. SOUTHWORTH

RICHARD KAY
80 SLEAFORD ROAD, BOSTON, LINCOLNSHIRE PE21 8EU

In accordance with the requirements
of the Copyright, Designs and Patents Act 1988
Pamela A. Southworth has asserted her right
to be regarded as the author of this work.

© Pamela A. Southworth 2005
First published by Richard Kay Publications 2005
ISBN 1 902882 56 3

All rights reserved. No part of this publication may be reproduced, stored in a retrieval system, nor transmitted in any form other than that in which it is now published, nor by any means, mechanical, electronic, photocopying, nor by any other means, except for brief extracts in written reviews, without the prior permission of the publisher in writing.

Printed and bound in England by Foxe Graphics Ltd.,
Enterprise Road, Golf Road Industrial Estate,
MABLETHORPE, Lincolnshire LN12 1NB

ACKNOWLEDGEMENTS

I would like to thank the staff at the Essex Archives for their help in finding out about the fire in Delaney's boarding house, *Thompson's Weekly News* for allowing me to quote from Delaney's own story, Dorothy Kemp for her dedication when we kept drawing a blank with various lines of enquiry, and lastly my thanks to Robert Vink who did much of the research for this book, and whose encouragement led me to write it.

DELANEY THE CAT BURGLAR

INTRODUCTION

Delaney was the original 'cat-burglar' – the phrase was said to have been coined for him. He was very fit and agile and thought nothing of shinning up a drain pipe to gain entrance to the houses he intended to burgle. His *modus opperandi* shook the police in London and for a while he puzzled them, as they couldn't think how he had entered the premises. He would balance himself on the window-sill whilst opening the window, as sure footed as any feline – hence the term 'cat-burglar'. To open the window he carried what he termed his 'gadget', a tool he described as having been fashioned from 'a common household item'. He was wanted by New Scotland Yard and featured in their Rogues Gallery. After he was caught the newspapers described him as a swell mobsman[1], because he was always stylishly dressed and had a distinguished appearance.

Delaney's story has been difficult to write as he told so many lies it was not easy to decide just what the truth was. This led to our following some wrong leads. He claimed to have been educated by the Jesuits in Capetown. After much combing of the internet and many emails later, I discovered that there were no Jesuits in Capetown when he was living in South Africa. His age changed to suit the circumstances he found himself in, and even his name, which he always gave as Robert Augustus Delaney, was in fact Aloysious, not Augustus.

In his 'own story' written for *Thomson's Weekly News* in 1934, he started by saying that he was born in 1895 in Cape Town. It proved impossible to confirm this and it was finally established that he had in fact been born in Dublin some four years earlier than he claimed. This was discovered when his army record came into my possession. Almost every avenue we followed drew a blank, but with some diligent detective work, enough information has come to light to get a picture of Delaney and recognise him as the con man he truly was.

---

[1] Oxford English Dictionary: *Swell mob, a class of pickpockets who assumed the dress and manners of respectable people in order to escape detection.* [Slang. Now Obs. Or Hist first dated usage 1836]

CHAPTER ONE

The Beginnings

Robert Augustus Delaney was (according to various newspapers) born in Capetown, South Africa, on 12th June 1895. However on his service record it states that he was born in Dublin in 1891. This could possibly be the truth as he claimed to be the son of an Irishman, Charles Peter Delaney, who according to Robert 'left the auld country' for South Africa. Charles Delaney was supposedly a civil engineer, though on his marriage certificate Robert described his father as a jeweller. However his parents seem to have lived in affluent circumstances in a 'little place about eight miles from the Cape'. According to Robert Delaney his mother was a Boer lady, and he described his father as 'a landowner'.

Robert Delaney wasn't exceptionally tall, being only five foot nine inches, and was a lightly built young man with light auburn wavy hair, blue eyes and a charming manner, which he soon learnt to use to his advantage. He had impeccable manners and was very attractive to the opposite sex. He could also spin a plausible story in a most believable manner and had no qualms about telling lies if it suited him. He had all the makings of a 'con-man'.

Young Robert supposedly had a good education, culminating in a trip to England in 1914 with enough money to take him to university. He later claimed to have been to Jesus College, Cambridge, which however was quite untrue. One story has him spending his allowance on 'sowing his wild oats' in London, and when it had all gone he was said to have joined the army.

However we do know the latter to be true as on the third of August 1915, in Potchepstroon, South Africa, Robert Delaney enlisted for the duration of the war, to serve in the South African Heavy Artillery. He had been part of the Cape Garrison Artillery until it had been disbanded. On the enlistment papers he gave his name as Robert Aloysious Delaney, described himself as a tailor's cutter and gave his birth place as Dublin. He stated that he had resided away from his father's house for at least three years and had never been in trouble with the police! He was twenty four years old and he gave his sister, Mrs P Hill, as his next of kin, suggesting that his parents were both dead. (In 1934 when writing his story for *Thomson's Weekly News* he said his mother was still alive!)

Robert was posted to England and was stationed at Cooden Camp, near Bexhill-on-Sea. Delaney would have us believe that his army record was good and that he quickly rose to the rank of sergeant. He claimed to have seen service in East and West Africa, Egypt and France, where he fought in Armentiers and in the Battle of the Somme. He also claimed to have been wounded in 'a liquid fire attack' and was consequently sent back to England, where he had a spell in hospital in Salisbury. The only spell in hospital he had in England was when, on arriving at Cooden Camp, it was found that he had venereal disease.

After this he said he 'followed the example of many overseas soldiers by getting married'. Delaney was not averse to stretching the truth for the sake of a good story, and it shows here, for in the autumn of 1915, Delaney had met Kitty Sharpe, a wealthy widow from Swineshead. What lies he told her we will never know but after a very brief courtship they were married. The marriage certificate shows that they were married on the eleventh of December 1915. He certainly didn't see any action in the Battle of the Somme, for it took place between July and November 1916 and Delaney was declared a deserter on the third of January 1916!

* * *

Kate Sharpe (also known as Kitty) was born in 1879. She was the fourth daughter of John Harrison Brown, a wealthy farmer of 223 acres, who also owned a brick and tile factory in Swineshead Fenhouses. He employed thirty-seven men and eleven boys, and was a wealthy man. Kate was used to a life of luxury, with servants to wait on her and a live-in nanny/governess who looked after her and her four sisters, Eleanor, Ada, Alice and Bertha. Bertha never married but lived at home with her mother until she died in 1919, but Kitty's other sisters all married and the *Guardian & Independent* newspaper on January 4th 1896 carried a report of the wedding of Eleanor Elizabeth Brown, Kitty's eldest sister. Eleanor married Herbert Westaby Smith from Sutterton, and the wedding was a very grand affair with guests from many local families. The church path was carpeted for the occasion and the list of wedding presents was impressive. It was clear that the family were wealthy.

Rather strangely Eleanor was given away by her father's cousin, Ebenezer Wilson. Mr Brown was still alive at this time, as he didn't die until three years later when, whilst on holiday in Bournemouth, he died suddenly of influenza. He was fifty six and his sudden death would have been a great shock to both Mrs Brown and her daughters. He left £42,275, which, in today's terms would have been over two million pounds.

John Brown was well known throughout Lincolnshire as a grower of fruit of all kinds. Some years earlier he had planted orchards of apple, pear and plum trees, as well as acres of soft fruit. When he died one of his employees, a seedsman called Joel Goodwin, took over the business. Joel Goodwin employed a young man called William Gilding, who had been the foreman/manager for John Brown. Gilding later became a partner in the firm, eventually taking over after Mr Goodwin's early death. Some years later Delaney was to burgle William Gilding's offices in Fenhouses, in effect robbing the business that had once belonged to his father-in-law!

However, at the time of her father's death, Kate was engaged to be married to a local farmer, Joshua Sharpe, (also known as Frank). Kate and Joshua were married on 4th December of that year (1899). He was the youngest of a large family, having five older brothers and two sisters. His father, also Joshua Sharpe, farmed in and around Bicker, as well as owning a brewery at Hoffleet Stowe. Kitty was just twenty, having celebrated her birthday four weeks earlier on 29th September, and her spouse was twenty-one. The witnesses included Ebenezer Wilson, who probably gave the bride away in place of her late father.

Frank and Kitty lived a comfortable life, and eventually moved to a large house in Woodhall Spa, called *'Harewood'*. It was here that Frank died suddenly and unexpectedly of a heart attack whilst walking in his garden talking to his farm manager. He was only thirty-four years old and he and Kitty had been married for thirteen years. Unfortunately they had had no family and so, in order that Kate was not alone, one of her nieces came to live with her and stayed to become her companion. Kate would probably have been accompanied by this girl when she took the tour which resulted in her hasty marriage to Delaney.

Her husband's death was a great shock to Mrs Sharpe and, so the story goes, to get over the trauma of so suddenly losing her

CERTIFIED COPY of an **ENTRY OF MARRIAGE** Pursuant to the Marriage Act 1949

Registration District: Battle

15. Marriage solemnized at Eye Register Office in the District of Battle in the County of Sussex

When Married.	Name and Surname.	Age.	Condition.	Rank or Profession.	Residence at the time of Marriage.	Father's Name and Surname.	Rank or Profession
Eleventh December 1915	Robert Augustus Delaney	24 years	Bachelor	Gunner 78 Siege Battery Royal Garrison Artillery	Loader Camp Bexhill	Charles Peter Delaney (deceased)	Jeweller
	Kate Sharpe	36 years	Widow	Tailor Cutter	18 Albert Road Bexhill	John Harrison Brown (deceased)	Farmer

Married in the Register Office according to the Rites and Ceremonies of the _____ by Licence

In the presence of us:
G. J. Orpett
W. J. Luscombe

A. D. Gurr
Kate Sharpe

Registrar
Superintendent Registrar

'Crossgates' also known as **'The Limes'**, where Delaney and his wife Kitty lived for a few years before Delaney sold it to Mr. Charles Collins before leaving for London and Westcliffe-on-Sea with Kitty's niece.
(Courtesy of Alan East)

husband she hired a chauffeur and set off to tour the country, staying in expensive hotels. In November of that year she arrived in Bexhill on Sea, where she met Delaney. It didn't take him long to realise she was a very wealthy widow. Her husband had left her £22,000 and she had also inherited £8,000 when her father had died. This made her a very attractive prospect for Delaney and he set out to gain her confidence and charm her into marriage. A month later on the 11th December 1915 they were married at Battle, in Sussex. Kate was aged thirty six and Delaney was twenty four.

However, there are some discrepancies in this tale, as Joshua Sharpe died on 21st April 1912 and Delaney and Kate were not married until December 1915. This means that Kitty had been a widow for at least three and a half years.

Kitty Delaney would always have been dependant on the man in her life – firstly her father, and later her first husband – and would possibly not have been used to making her own decisions, as women were not so independent in those days. Having been cosseted and protected all her life by the men in her life, what more natural than she would expect to do the same with her second husband. Delaney had no difficulty in persuading Kitty to sign over the management of her finances to him once they were married. Her money was invested in various farms around Lincolnshire, but once he gained control of his wife's estate, Delaney converted her assets to ready cash and began his spending spree.

At first the newly-weds lived in Woodhall Spa, at *Harewood*, the house she had shared with her first husband. It is not clear how long they lived there, but very soon Delaney was purchasing 'one of the finest farms' in Lincolnshire. He spent £22,500 on buying *The Limes* (at other times known as *Crossgates*) and the farmland that went with it, and Kitty and her charming husband came to live in Swineshead.

Robert Delaney knew nothing about farming, but was heard to boast more than once that he could learn all he needed to know about the job in six months. Colin Smith, whose father owned the mill at Swineshead North End, relates a story of how Delaney purchased two tons of cattle cake from him to feed his one solitary cow. This caused much merriment among the residents of Swineshead. It wasn't long before Delaney decided to hire a farm manager.

At some point in his marriage to Kitty, Delaney brought a boy to live with them at *The Limes,* a boy whom he described as his brother

Willie. Willie was sent to school in Skegness to a weekly boarding school. Also at this school was another boy from Swineshead, Norman Holland, whose father kept the local grocery store. Norman and Willie became quite friendly and sometimes Willie would stay over with Norman at weekends, mostly when Robert was away. As suddenly as he had appeared, Willie was whisked off to London, supposedly to further his education, and nothing more was ever heard of him. This created much speculation amongst the residents of Swineshead, especially in the light of later events when Delaney was known to be training boys to help him with his burglaries.

Delaney soon became bored with farming and took to more sporting activities. He acquired a gun and a dog, bought himself a 'hunter' or two, and was often to be seen out enjoying himself. But the other farmers in Swineshead didn't take kindly to Robert, having recognised him for what he truly was, a braggart and a wastrel. They would gladly have helped and advised him (his hunters were of dubious pedigree as he knew nothing of horse flesh) and shared their farming knowledge, but Robert Delaney was too arrogant and boastful for their liking. They very soon had enough of him and he found it necessary to go further afield to make friends. Consequently he found himself often seeking hospitality in Donington, where he met various young ladies who caught his roving eye. He was rumoured to be paying court to more than one woman.

By this time Kitty was probably beginning to realise what she had done by marrying Robert Delaney. He was spending her money, neglecting her for other women and generally ruining her life by bringing disgrace upon her. In the summer of 1922 she had a nervous breakdown, and had to go away to recuperate. Opinion in the village was that Delaney was trying to get his wife certified in order to be rid of her.

On her return she found that her estate had been sold to pay her husband's debts. The farm and livestock, the house and their two cars, had all gone. *The Limes* and its 170 acres of land for which Delaney had paid £22,000 was sold for only £17,000, two cars costing over £600 were sold for £250, and his so called 'hunters', supposedly worth £100 each, made only £20 a head. However, undaunted, Delaney was preparing to leave for London.

Before he left Robert told Kitty he was leaving her to go away with her niece. He gave his wife £20 and a promise of some more money later. This, of course, never materialised. In fact some of the older residents of Swineshead tell a story of Delaney actually visiting Kitty in later years to ask her to give him money! Poor Mrs Delaney! She had gone from being a wealthy widow to a deserted wife in the space of a few years. Destitute, she had to begin to earn her own living for the first time in her life. She worked first of all in a hotel in Boston and later was in service at Wisbech. After the death of her mother in 1925, Kitty lived in a small cottage on Cheese Hill, in the centre of Swineshead, which was left to her in her mother's will. Kitty's mother also left her a small annuity on which Kitty was able to live. In 1958 Kitty sold this cottage to Frank Horn, the local barber, and moved in to a council bungalow in Bullen's Lane. Her little cottage on Cheese Hill was demolished and replaced by Frank's new barber's shop. A baker's shop now stands on this site.

And what of Delaney? When he left Swineshead he boasted that he would soon reclaim his fortune - but that was not to be. He in fact left the village where he was not much liked and went south to embark on a new career that would eventually bring him to the attention of New Scotland Yard!

The little cottage on Cheese Hill in which Kitty Delaney lived for some years after Delaney left her almost penniless.

CHAPTER TWO

London

It was in the autumn of 1922 that Delaney and Kitty's niece left Swineshead and headed south. They were next heard of in Westcliffe-on-Sea, where they were said to have purchased a bed and breakfast establishment for £1,500. In actual fact the premises belonged to Mr Ainslie of 24 Martins Lane, Cannon Street, London. Delaney either rented or leased the property. It was quite a grand establishment, known as *Beech House*, and was situated on the corner of Hamlet Court Road and Ditton Court Road. It was described as having 140 feet of frontage on Hamlet Court Road and about the same length on Ditton Court Road, and a five foot right of way at the rear. It contained seven bedrooms on the first floor, two more on the top floor plus a very long room which may originally have been servants quarters. Downstairs there were four reception rooms, a large hall, a kitchen, a pantry, and a scullery with a tradesman's entrance. The back garden was well laid out with a flower garden and a fruit and vegetable garden. There were also some green houses.

Delaney settled down to running this boarding house with Kitty's niece, whom he now described as his wife. However this phase of their life didn't last long, as on Wednesday 15th March 1923 there was a fire at this boarding house causing extensive damage. Delaney awoke around 4am to the smell of smoke, and on opening his bedroom door saw flames coming from the dining room. He rushed up to the second floor to arouse three women guests and one of them, Miss J Anderson, ran to telephone the fire brigade, who were swiftly on the scene. Before they arrived a passing policeman, PC Howard, entered the premises to search the building for anyone who might have been trapped, but everyone escaped unhurt.

The boarding house adjoined a shop belonging to '*Curzon Brothers, Clothiers and Outfitters*', a well known firm with two shops in the town. The manager of this shop, Mr Philip Cohen, and his wife occupied a flat, which was also attached to Delaney's guest house, and it was feared that the flat and the shop would be destroyed too. However the firemen soon had the blaze under control, but Delaney's dining room which was on the first floor, was completely burned out, and the fire having spread up to the large room on the second floor,

The boarding house that Delaney ran for a while with Kitty's niece. This shot shows what would have been the tailor's shop adjoining. The building was rebuilt after the fire.

(Photo by Robert Vink, 2002.)

Another view of Delaney's boarding house in Westcliffe-on-Sea showing the full frontage on to Ditton Court Road.
(Photo by Robert Vink, 2002.)

the entire roof had caved in. The newspaper reported that 'valuable furs, linen, and travelling trunks' were destroyed by the fire, and the cause was thought to be a faulty stove situated in the dining room.

Delaney tried to claim £2,000 from the insurance company, but only received £400.

Possibly by now disillusioned with Delaney, having seen him at much closer quarters, Kitty's niece decided to return home. Delaney may possibly have been truly fond of this girl, as he seems to have been quite upset. He placed an advertisement in a London newspaper asking her to communicate with him, in which he described her as his wife, though there was no evidence of their ever having married. In fact there is no evidence that Kitty and Robert Delaney were ever divorced, thus freeing him to remarry. Finding out that Kitty's niece had returned home, Delaney travelled up to Swineshead to fetch her back, but her family would not allow him to see her. It was said that they 'hid her away' until he had left. Disappointed, Delaney returned to London.

Assuming the name 'Captain Craddock', Delaney lived in the West End of London for a while in various expensive hotels. To pay his bills he resorted to crime. This apparently was not the first time he had broken the law. On his constant visits to London whilst still living with Kitty, it seems he may have done various 'jobs' in the smarter areas of the metropolis. He went up to town for some nightlife and excitement, which he found in his own inimitable way.

He had always been fit and agile and when living in Swineshead he had played cricket and football for the local teams. He had also displayed a certain ability to 'climb like a squirrel'. In an article written many years later for a London newspaper, Delaney claimed to have learned to shin up and down drainpipes as a boy at the Convent of St Joseph's, where he claimed to have been educated by the Jesuits. He said he had had a lot of practice escaping out of his bedroom window to visit cinemas and theatres at night. Climbing up a drainpipe to gain access through an upstairs window would have presented no problems to Robert Delaney! This was an innovative method of house breaking and new to the police at that time, and they couldn't work out at first how it was done. When they discovered his method of entry, they described the thief as a 'cat-burglar'.

His *modus operandi* was simple. He mixed with society ladies, made a note of the jewellery they wore, and at a later date went to their home, climbed up the drain pipes and entered by an upstairs window. He carried in his pocket what he termed his 'gadget', with which he opened the windows. He would get to know one of the maids, ply her with alcoholic drinks and even seduce her if necessary, in order to find out the plan of the house and where the girl's mistress kept her jewels. Such was his confidence that, with the jewels in his pockets, he would sometimes leave by the front door! It seems that during his marriage to Kitty, Delaney had often made visits to London to 'see his salesman', but was in reality living it up frequenting night clubs and making friends with society ladies. He may have tried his hand at burglary even then.

Delaney had considerable success with this way of life for some time. Enough time in fact to steal sufficient money for a holiday touring the Balkans, Austria and Czechoslovakia. It was during this period that he may have associated with some members of the Parisian underworld. On his return to England, Delaney purchased an electro-plating plant in London, but he was allegedly no more successful at this than any of the other legitimate ventures he had tried. Anything requiring real work was not to his taste. He preferred 'easy money'. He decided to change his name again, this time calling himself Lane.

Back to his old tricks, his confidence ran away with him and he began forging cheques. At this point in his career Delaney was sharing a flat with a man named Ernest Roebuck. The two of them went on a spending spree in Kensington, buying among other things some tins of a particular brand of salmon, and paying with a worthless cheque. Detectives searching his dustbins found the empty tins. These were used as evidence against him. Delaney immediately filed for bankruptcy, but failed to turn up at court for the hearing.

On September 25th 1924, Delaney and Roebuck appeared at Westminster Police Court charged with 'uttering forged cheques'. Some facts emerged at this trial. Apparently Delaney had at some time been associated with both Australian and African criminals, though no details were given. Also he had recently been charged with living on the immoral earnings of a woman. When this point was brought up at the trial he objected strongly, as he had been found 'not guilty' on that count. Roebuck received a sentence of six months imprisonment. However despite the evidence, Delaney put his charm to good use and persuaded the magistrate to deal with him as a first offender. He was bound over in the sum of £10 for twelve months to come up for judgement if called upon. In his summing up the judge said that he hoped that Delaney would use his talents, acrobatic or otherwise, to lead an honest life in future.

He wasn't so lucky the next time. In February 1925, he appeared at Marlborough Street Police Court on various charges. Between December 27th and 29th of the previous year he had entered 25 St James' Place, London, the home of Lady Northcote, where he had stolen a diamond and amethyst brooch and some letters and documents. On January 15th he tried to enter the residence of the Duke of Rutland in Arlington Street, W1. However, Delaney was by now under surveillance, and as he left the premises he was chased by the police. Trying to hide from them, he was finally apprehended in the grounds of the Overseas Club in Park Place, St James'. Detective Sergeant Symes, who caught Delaney, said the prisoner had on him a table knife with a piece chipped out along the edge of the blade. He said a small piece of steel had been found on the floor by the window that matched the damaged blade. When charged Delaney said: *'I don't want my friends to know where I am. I wish to clear everything up. Let my young lady know where I am. I have been living with her at Park Road for a fortnight in the name of Lane. You will find all the documents sealed in a parcel in the cloakroom at Piccadilly Circus Tube Station. They are of no use to anybody except Baroness Northcote. I pawned her brooch at Hampsted Road for £10 and the jemmy I broke into the house with I bought for three shillings. I will help you all I can.'* Perhaps Delaney was trying to co-operate with the police in order to escape prison. If this was so, it didn't work. For these crimes he was sent down for three and a half years.

CHAPTER THREE

Delaney's Own Story

Delaney's version of events differs in many ways. Some years later, no doubt in need of the money, Delaney wrote his story for the newspapers. An article appeared in *Thomson's Weekly News*, in which he boasted that there wasn't a prison in England that he couldn't have escaped from had he wished to. He said he realised that gaol-breakers always got caught and wishing to leave with a clean sheet, he decided to stay inside and complete his term.

He described his earlier life with his wealthy wife, and said that when differences arose between them he left the country, reaching Paris with £30,000 in his pocket. He claimed to have taken only three months to spend this money, during which time he travelled from Paris to Brussels, Vienna and Prague. Having hit the high spots, drinking, gambling and generally living it up, Delaney found himself back in Paris, but this time penniless. He described his situation: '*I stood in my rooms in the hotel and turned out my pockets. Not a bean. I was dead broke.*' Three days later, hungry and desperate, he fell in with a group of men, some English and some American, who persuaded him to work for them. They got him a job as a dancing partner in a club, where he was to get to know the wealthy ladies and make notes as to their jewels, where they lived and when they would be out. He passed on this information to the men, who later stole these jewels and paid Delaney his share of the proceeds. He never knew any of the details of the robbery, but as long as they paid him he was not interested. However, he soon realised that he could do this himself without the gang, and decided to start on his own. To this end he returned to London.

Within two weeks he had made himself known to most of the society ladies on the dance floors of all the big London hotels, and was soon being invited to their homes. The women made a big fuss of him and although he described himself as being far from happy, he said he couldn't see any other way of making a living other than by becoming a 'gentleman burglar'!

Delaney went on to describe his first job in London. His victim was a middle aged titled lady whom he met in a West End hotel. Delaney described her as '*one of those women anxious to have the last kick out of life before it was too late,'* and said he *'played up to her'* for all he was worth. She invited him to lunch the next day, and they went on to dance at one of the fashionable clubs and later she allowed him to escort her home. He was invited to tea the next afternoon. Delaney became a regular visitor to this woman's home, eventually finding out where she kept her jewels, which he learned were insured for a large sum. He watched the house for a couple of nights wondering how to go about it.

Whilst watching the upper windows he remembered how, as a schoolboy, he had climbed up and down the stack pipe to get in and out of his bedroom without being seen. He was excited by the idea. He wrote: *'So far as I knew, this was something new in burglary in this country – why not have a shot at it? There was an element of sport in it which appealed to me.'*

The next night about seven o'clock he put on his dress suit, set his opera hat on the back of his head and checked his appearance in the mirror. Satisfied with what he saw, he made himself one of his gadgets for opening windows, put this in his pocket and went out to call a cab.

If we are to believe Robert Delaney this was his first job, although it is most unlikely that it would have been. However, he described it thus: *'The house was one of those old Georgian buildings, fronting a mews in which the occupants kept their limousines. Turning into this little courtyard I wasted no time, but still in my light dress overcoat, sprang at the low wall, got on the top, and, leaning over, caught hold of the stack pipe. It was quite firm. The lady of the house, I knew, was not at home, and as it was nearly the hour for dinner all the servants would be in the kitchen getting ready for the meal. Forty feet up were their bedrooms. They were all in darkness, and as I started to climb I made up my mind that it would be easier to enter by one of these top windows. The climb did not present any great difficulties. The toes of my evening dress shoes were very supple, and allowed me to get a good leverage on the wall. Tightening my grip on the pipe, I found that I had lost nothing of the prowess of my boyhood days. Foot by foot I worked my way up, till at last I was at the top. One mistake and I would have crashed to certain death on the concrete below. I got one foot on the ledge of the window and swung myself over. This accomplished, I steadied myself, loosened one hand, got out my little* gadget, and slid back the catch of the window. Next moment I was inside.

Feeling my way round the room – I carried no torch – I found the door, got on to the servants landing, and listened. Not a sound. I cannot say that I have any particular sensations to describe about this first job. I certainly had no fear. I simply walked downstairs and turned the handle of my lady's bedroom, walked in, and helped myself to her gee-gaws. They were in her jewel case in a corner cupboard. I knew where the keys were kept, and I opened the case, filled my pockets with the jewels and walked out again. Once outside I listened again and heard no sounds. Pausing at the head of the stairs to light a cigarette, I walked down, opened the front door of the house in the absence of the butler, and walked along the street. I hailed a taxi and drove straight back to my hotel.'

Back in his hotel room Robert checked his haul. There were diamonds, pearls, emerald rings, necklaces and brooches. His only worry now was how to dispose of them. He remembered hearing the gang he worked for in Paris talking of a certain Kammy Grizzard, who was supposedly the biggest fence in London. He looked him up in the telephone book. He arranged to meet him the following evening and was given £600 for a string of pearls. Kammy Grizzard also gave Delaney some advice. He told him to work alone, as detectives would not find him out but informers would give him away. Delaney must have heeded his advice for he said: 'By living as a man about town and keeping myself to myself I had a long run. But it was a very enterprising young 'tec who rumbled me in the end and sent me away.'

Delaney was finally caught after robbing Lady Northcote. Amongst his haul were documents and letters described by the press as 'instructions in the event of death', but Delaney's version is more romantic. If we can believe all that he had to say in this article, the documents he stole from Lady Northcote were love letters. When he realised what he had stolen Delaney said: 'To a man of my upbringing and outlook I may as well say that this gave me a shock. There are some things in life which are sacred even to a burglar. You may not credit it, but he has his code of morals like any other man or woman, and I felt that if it were not for the risk, I would have liked to have gone straight back, climbed the stack pipe, and put that envelope back where I found it.' He felt that he really shouldn't read them as they were of such a personal nature - but he opened them none the less! The love letters were from what he presumed to be a young man. They were full of passion and romance and Delaney could not put them down. He said *'the writer was evidently a young man, and his love had inspired him to put all his soul into words that filled me with the glow of romance.'*

When he had read them all Robert Delaney suddenly felt a pang of conscience. He said of himself *'What had I done. I was not only a burglar, but a cad.'* This apparently made him feel miserable. He sat down to reflect on the situation. Being a romantic at heart he felt for the lady and he decided to return the letters, but how? The following day, Sunday, he went out for a walk to mull over the situation. He left the envelope locked in his safe.

Whilst walking along Piccadilly he met a famous detective from Scotland Yard (he did not name him), who stopped him and struck up a conversation. He introduced himself, but Delaney pretended not to have heard of him, despite having recognised him. The detective clearly knew who Delaney was. Having introduced himself, the man proceeded to tell Delaney of the previous night's burglary. He explained that some valuable papers had been stolen and should they be returned the owner would perhaps overlook the theft of the jewels. The conversation was a charade, Delaney acting the innocent, and the detective acting as if he were suspicious of Delaney, who felt that he was being warned that they were aware of him at last. Back in his room he wiped the letters with a cloth in an effort to clean off any fingerprints and put them back in their envelope to return them. About 8 o'clock that night he left his flat and walking along Shaftsbury Avenue he hailed a taxi to take him to the lady's house. He alighted some way from the house and checking to see if he had been observed, he crossed the road and posted the letters through the letter-box. Not realising that he had in fact been seen, he walked away and hailed another cab to return home. He would have liked to gain entry and put the letters back in their original place but felt that would have been too dangerous.

The newspapers next day were full of the burglary, detailing the jewels and money, but not mentioning the letters. For the next week or so Delaney scanned the newspapers for a 'thank you' message in the agony columns expecting to get an acknowledgement of his 'kind deed' in returning them. But nothing of the kind materialised. He sold the jewels for what he described as *'quite a good little sum'*, and lived on the proceeds for a month or two.

The police may have suspected him, but they did nothing about it. Full of confidence that he had got away with it Delaney planned his next job, but he was now under surveillance and his every move was being monitored. On January 15th 1925 Delaney attempted to break into the residence of the Duke of Rutland in Arlington Street, W1. Something went wrong with this attempted break-in and Delaney had to make a hasty escape by climbing over a wall. He was finally apprehended in the grounds of The Overseas Club in Park Place, St James'. Caught at last, Delaney was sent to prison.

CHAPTER FOUR

Swineshead

Delaney was released early on licence from this first sentence, and he next comes to our attention in 1927, when he came once more to Swineshead. Apparently he had always harboured a grievance against William Gilding when he was living at Swineshead with Kitty. Mr Gilding was a seedsman, potato merchant and fruit grower, in Swineshead Fenhouses, and he had taken over this business from Mr Joel Goodwin, who had bought the business after Kitty Delaney's father died in 1899. In one of the articles he wrote for *Thomson's Weekly News* Delaney described this job as having been planned with a view to *'getting my own back'*. Getting his own back for what, he doesn't say.

It was a very windy Friday night in October when Robert Delaney and his accomplice, who went by the name of John Brown, arrived in Swineshead. Delaney had met this man in Parkhurst prison, where they had become friends. They had been released at almost the same time, and very soon formed a plan of action together which included a visit to Swineshead. They drove up from London in a stolen car, which they abandoned close to a shed in Fendyke Lane, Bicker. Delaney knew of this shed because it had been on his land when he had lived at *The Limes* with Kitty.

Delaney and Brown must then have walked to *The Limes*, which at that time was occupied by Mr Charles Collins. In his garage Mr Collins had an Austin 12hp saloon car which he thought he had safely locked away before going to bed the previous evening. However, nothing was safe when Delaney was about, and the next morning Mr Collins found his garage door had been forced and his car stolen.

Having stolen the car, Delaney and Brown drove to Swineshead Fenhouses to the offices of Messrs William Gilding Ltd. Matthew Henry Smith, clerk to William Gilding, later gave evidence to say that the offices had been securely fastened at 5.30pm the day before. To gain entry Delaney had had to break one window and force another.

Delaney's version is that he opened the safe in a very short time as he had been taught the art of safe breaking by some 'old lags' when he was in prison. In reality he failed to open the safe whilst still in the offices. Delaney and his accomplice carried the safe out to the car, placed it on the back seat along with a typewriter, a double barrelled gun and six cartridges, a gent's overcoat and a Boston Hospital collecting box. They drove back to Bicker to the shed in Fendyke Lane, where they used a pickaxe to break open the safe before abandoning it. Inside the safe were four banker's cheques, a cheque book containing two hundred and thirty six cheques, one hundred and twenty two health insurance stamps, a pocket wallet, twenty two title deeds, a partnership agreement, and a sale agreement. The total value of the stolen goods came to £6,277.6s.

This must have been in the early hours of the morning, as two gentlemen travelling towards Lincoln discovered Delaney and Brown sitting in their car in a ditch by Aswarby corner, on what is now known as the A15. The road still bends sharply just there. A tree had blown down in the gales that night causing them to run off the road. It was four o'clock in the morning. These two men, on their arrival in Sleaford, notified the police and PC Shaw was sent to investigate the matter. PC Allen, who was stationed at Osbournby, a village just south of the accident, also attended the scene. PC Allen was somewhat suspicious of Delaney and Brown as they were not dressed in the manner he would have expected of the owner of the quality of car they were driving. Neither was he satisfied with the answers Delaney gave him when questioned about the incident.

PC Allen suggested he go for help to pull the vehicle out of the dyke, and went to a nearby farm where he telephoned his superior officer, Inspector Collison. He then asked the farmer to lend his horses to pull the car from the ditch, but asked him to take his time about it thus giving the Inspector time to arrive. The farmer co-operated by managing to get the car further into the ditch. When Inspector Collison arrived he questioned Delaney who said the car was his and he was on his way to Peterborough on business. When asked his name Delaney replied *'Mr Collins, Swineshead,'* and he introduced Brown as Mr Wise.

Having some doubts about Delaney's story, and also noting the typewriter and gun on the back seat, the Inspector asked the two men to come with him to the police station for further questioning. He put his prisoners in the back of the car with PC Allen in charge of them, and he sat in the front next to the driver. They drove off without further incident but on approaching the railway crossing in Sleaford the gates closed and the car came to a halt. Delaney immediately

Gilding's offices as they look today (2002).
(Courtesy of Lorraine Whalley)

The window in Gilding's offices through which Delaney entered on the night of the robbery.

The shed where Delaney and Brown forced open William Gilding's safe.
Delaney had once owned both the shed and the land on which it stood.
(Photo by the author, 2002)

Photograph of Bicker Fen showing how isolated the shed was in the clump of
trees. The shed is just discernible to the right of the trees.
(Photo by Robert Vink 2002)

brandished a revolver (which was later found not to be loaded) and Brown began to kick PC Allen in the ribs. Some cars at that time had small drop down seats which when in use would face the people sitting on the back seat. This was probably the scenario here causing PC Allen to sit facing the prisoners. Inspector Collison jumped out of the front of the car and into the back to assist the constable and after a struggle, during which Inspector Collison received a black eye, Delaney and Brown were overpowered. They were eventually locked up at Sleaford police station. Later that day the two men were handed over to Boston County Police and were remanded in custody.

Delaney and Brown appeared before a special sitting of the North Holland magistrates at Boston Sessions House on 4th November. It was held in a small room on the ground floor usually assigned to the Magistrate's Clerk. It was too small to admit the public and was very cramped with just the officials and witnesses. Even so the safe the prisoners had stolen was in evidence in the room as was the double barrelled gun and various other exhibits. The Austin motor car they had stolen was parked outside. The safe was ordered to be taken outside to make more room for the magistrates, who that day were Messrs GL Nussey, C. Wright and J. Brown.

The prisoners tried to look as nonchalant as possible, Delaney lounging against the wall and Brown against the bookcase. Brown was wearing a blue serge suit and had a black and blue scarf hanging around his neck. Delaney was wearing a brown raincoat buttoned up to the chin. The two men were charged with breaking and entering the garage of Charles Collins, of The Limes, Swineshead, and stealing his Austin saloon motor car valued at £300, on 29th October 1927. They were also charged with breaking and entering the offices of William Gilding Ltd, Swineshead and stealing a safe, a gun, six cartridges, a gentleman's overcoat, a typewriter and a Boston Hospital collecting box containing thirty shillings. Delaney pleaded guilty to being in possession of the car but denied breaking into Gilding's offices. Brown pleaded not guilty to both charges.

Inspector Collison gave his evidence followed by Sergeant Dobson, the policeman who escorted the prisoners from Sleaford to Boston. Sergeant Dobson said that on the morning of the 30th October he had gone to the offices of Mr William Gilding and made an examination of the scene of the crime. Later that day together with some other police officers he visited a shed in Bicker belonging to Mr

Charles Collins where he found the stolen safe which had been forced open. A pickaxe lay nearby and it seemed that this had been used to open the safe. The pointed end of the axe and the holes in the safe matched. A Morris Oxford car, registration number PE 3994, was parked on the opposite side of the road to this shed. This car may have been used by the prisoners on their journey up to Lincolnshire.

Charles Collins, whose car had been stolen presumably to replace the Morris Oxford, then described how he had put his car away the night before and discovered it missing the next morning at 6.30am. His evidence was followed by that of Matthew Henry Smith, a clerk in the employ of William Gilding Ltd, who stated that when he left the office on the evening of 28th October, all the windows were securely closed and the door locked. The next morning at 7am he discovered one of the windows broken and an office stool lying on the ground outside the window. The door was still locked, but on entering the office he saw papers strewn around the floor, drawers open in the desks, the blind torn down and books removed from their usual places. The office was in general disorder. He then found that a safe was missing from the other room, at which point he notified Mr Gilding.

Gilbert Arthur Johnson, managing director of William Gilding Ltd then identified the chequebooks and other items that were in the stolen safe. Having done so he said that the total value of the stolen property was £6,277 6s.

The next witness was Ernest Clayton, manager for William Gilding Ltd. He said he had left his double barrel gun and some cartridges in the office on the evening before the break-in and recognised the cartridges produced in evidence as being similar to those that were stolen. The stolen gun he estimated as being worth £12 but he said he had also lost an overcoat worth £4. At this point Mr Clayton was asked if his overcoat bore any resemblance to the one Delaney was wearing at present. He said it did and Delaney was requested to remove his coat for Mr Clayton to examine. Mr Clayton identified it as being his property. The Clerk to the Court then spoke saying this was most unusual as the coat should have been in the possession of the police. Since Mr Clayton was in no doubt that it was his, Delaney was forced to relinquish his overcoat.

While the magistrates were considering their verdict, Delaney and Brown were taken to another room. At this point it was found that numerous members of the public had crowded into the passageway of the Sessions House in order to get a glimpse of Delaney. The prisoners were finally committed for trial at the Derbyshire Assizes which were due to open on the following Monday. The reason for this was because of a new system by which Justices could commit cases to an assize in a neighbouring county to save time. This reform was designed to speed up the administration of justice.

It was on the following Wednesday that Delaney and Brown appeared before Mr Justice Swift at the Derbyshire Assizes. The Assizes had opened on the Monday with thirty prisoners on the calendar, twenty six from Derbyshire, three from Lincolnshire and one from Loughborough. Delaney was described as *'Robert Delaney, aged 32, an engineer'* and Brown was listed as *'John Brown, aged 23, a motor driver'.* They were both charged with: *'Breaking and entering a garage, in the occupation of Charles Collins, at Swineshead, and therein stealing an Austin saloon car, valued at £300, the property of Mr Collins, on or about 29th October. Also with breaking and entering the offices of William Gilding Ltd, at Swineshead, and therein stealing a safe, containing four banker's cheques, 239 National Health Insurance stamps, 236 blank banker's cheques, a pocket wallet, 22 title deeds, a partnership agreement and a sale agreement; also an Underwood typewriter, a double-barrel shotgun, six cartridges, a gent's overcoat, and a Boston Hospital collection box, together to the value of £6,277 6s.'*

The case was first called on Tuesday morning, when after the Grand Jury had been charged, Delaney and Brown were brought before His Lordship. It seems they had both written to apply for legal aid. His Lordship explained that he had considered their application carefully and had decided that this was not a case in which he could grant it. They would both have to make their own arrangements.

The case was eventually dealt with late on Wednesday afternoon. The court was crowded and many more were waiting outside to gain admission. During the case the both humorous and sarcastic remarks of Mr Justice Swift raised laughter in the court. At one point halfway through the proceedings when he asked if the safe was burglar proof, he had to threaten to clear the court if the audience didn't remain silent.

Mr W K Carter was the prosecuting barrister. He outlined the case to the jury describing the situation as we have seen above. It emerged that that the pickaxe used to open the safe was the property of Holland County Council, but no more information about the Morris motor car found near the shed in Bicker was given. The same witnesses were called as before to give their evidence. The *Boston Guardian* newspaper reported the trial and quoted the judge and witnesses verbatim:

'*His Lordship then asked how many men it would take to carry the safe into court.*
The witness Smith: Two strong men can carry it in.
The Judge: Well let two strong officers carry it in. (Laughter). Don't let it fall on your toes, officer. (More laughter). [The safe was brought in.]
The Judge addressing the Jury: I want you to see this safe because it is suggested that these two men, Delaney and Brown, carried it out of the offices and placed it in a motor car. You have to make up your minds whether or no they could have done this.
[Gilbert Arthur Johnson was next to give evidence]
The Judge: How much was the safe worth?
Witness: About £20.
Judge: Was it burglar proof? (Laughter).
Witness: No your Lordship.
It does not look like it, does it? asked his Lordship amid renewed laughter'.

Delaney, who seemed to be conducting his own defence, elected to go into the box to give evidence. He said: '*I left London by the four o'clock train in the afternoon from King's Cross. We reached Peterborough, myself and my friend Brown, about half past six. We stayed there about three hours, and then walked from there towards Sleaford. On the way, we came upon this motor car abandoned in the ditch, and upon examining it, found it belonged to an old friend of mine, Mr Collins. I also found some papers inside it, belonging to Mr Gilding. Both of these gentlemen I knew very well. I thought the best thing I could do was to have the car pulled out of the dyke, and take it back to Mr Collins, of Swineshead, and hand it back to him. We stopped a car coming down from Boston, and they said they could not assist us. They said they would report the matter to the Police when they reached Sleaford. Two hours afterwards, PC Allen came and said he could get someone to pull the car out for us. He did do this, and then the*

Inspector came up and said he was going to take us into custody while he made enquiries.
Mr Carter: Now just listen to me, Delaney. When the car was found in the dyke it was pointing towards London.
Delaney: It was pointing towards London and Peterborough. I found the car in the ditch, and I do not know how it got into the ditch.
When the Inspector came up did you say 'I am going to Peterborough on business?'
Yes I did say so.
You had just left there, had you not?
Yes.
Why did you tell the Inspector you were going to Peterborough on business? Why did you tell him the car was yours?
I had good reasons to tell him so.
His Lordship: How long have you known Mr Collins?
Delaney: I have known him eight or nine years. The farm he is now farming he bought off me.
Mr Carter: Did not you tell the Inspector Brown was employed by you? That is not true is it?
No.
What time did you find the car?
About four o'clock. We were there four and a half hours.
Where was the car going to that you stopped.
To Lincoln. They were going through Sleaford and I sent them to report the matter to the police there.
You said you were there four and a half hours and not one car passed you?
That is so.
What time did the constable come?
About 6 o'clock.
What was the object of yours?
I was taking Brown to Mr Dalton's at Swineshead to get him a job. We had no means to go by train.
The Judge: But you had the means to go from London to Peterborough, had you not?
Yes.
What made you start from London at 4 o'clock in the afternoon to go to Swineshead?
This question Delaney did not answer.

It seems very curious to me that when you took Brown to look for a job the same night someone broke into Mr Collin's garage, and Messrs Gilding's offices. It seems a little strange, does it not?
Yes, a little, my Lord.
Mr Carter: You were a little surprised, surely, when the policeman said he was going to arrest you?
Well, I was not surprised.
Why did you not tell Inspector Collison you were trying to get this car out for Mr Collins?
I had no reason to tell him so.
Why did you put a revolver against PC Allen's ribs?
Am I forced to answer that question?
The Judge: No, I don't think you need. Did you put the revolver in PC Allen's ribs?
Yes I did my Lord.'

Brown was next in the witness box. He corroborated Delaney's story, and agreed he was looking for a job as a tractor driver with a certain Mr J.P. Dalton, who was a friend of Delaney's. He said two men and a pair of horses came to pull the car out of the ditch.

Mr Carter: You say you were going to look for a job?
Yes.
Do you know this part of the country?
No, sir.
Do you know you were not on the direct road from Peterborough to Swineshead at all?
I do not know this road at all.
You know Delaney told the Inspector your name was Wise?
I did not hear him. I did not take any notice of what he said to him at all.
You did not take any interest at all then. I wonder whether you took any interest at all when you were arrested
I did not think there was any need to trouble.
You did not tell the Inspector that you were looking after the car that was Mr Collins'?
No, because he did not ask me.
And yet you started to kick the constable in the stomach when you reached Sleaford?

Yes, when he started to put his toes in my stomach.'

In summing up the Judge said the case was a very simple one. He asked the Jury to apply common sense when reaching their verdict. He reviewed the relevant facts and suggested that if these two men were really looking for work for Brown then they had no need of a revolver, unless they were going to try to force Dalton to give him a job! The Jury only took a few minutes to decide that they were both guilty as charged.

Delaney had only been discharged from prison on 14th October, just two weeks previous to committing this offence. He had been released early from his sentence, and as the Judge put it: *'He broke into this place while he was on a ticket-of-leave then?'* Brown, it seemed, was an Irishman whose real name was John O'Sullivan. He had been convicted in Ireland for felony on two occasions, once when he had stolen a motor car and another when he stole some cattle. He had also appeared at the Old Bailey in 1925 for robbery with possession of firearms, for which he had received a three year sentence. He had also been discharged early on licence in August, two months before Delaney, but disappeared from his job in London the same day that Delaney came out of gaol.

Delaney and Brown finally admitted to the charges and asked for two others to be taken into consideration. It seems that the abandoned Morris car found by the shed in Bicker had been left there by Delaney and Brown. They had stolen it from outside Kensington Court Mansions in London on 22nd October. That same night they had broken into a garage at St Neots in Huntingdonshire, where they stole twelve gallons of petrol and two overcoats. One of these coats was found in Brown's possession.

In sentencing the prisoners Mr Justice Swift said*: 'It is quite useless saying anything to you. You are dangerous motor thieves. You belong to the society that is so frequently found stealing motor cars and then using them to break into private places. You Delaney, have before been in penal servitude, and this time went on this expedition with a most dangerous weapon. The sentence of the Court upon you is that you be kept in penal servitude for seven years'.*

In sentencing Brown the judge said*: 'You are a younger man, and I am not sure that you are quite as wicked as Delaney, but I think you, this time, have been brought into this trouble through his influence.*

I shall not give you such a severe term of imprisonment. The sentence of the Court upon you is that you will be kept in penal servitude for three years. If it is possible, warder, please see that these men are sent to different prisons.
The Warder: I will have that done my Lord.'

The trial had lasted just over two hours.

* * *

Delaney decided to appeal and a Notice of Application for leave to Appeal, was registered on 10th November 1927. However, fifteen days later the Court of Appeal received a *'notice of Abandonment of all proceedings in regard to his appeal to the Court of Criminal Appeal.'* John Brown had also appealed and subsequently signed a Notice of Abandonment.

It is not known which prison John Brown was sent to, but Delaney served his time for this offence in Parkhurst. On 16th January 1930 the Governor of the prison noted that Delaney had registered a complaint against punishment received when he had a noisy dispute with another prisoner. He had started an argument with a prisoner named Gatzais whilst doing some repairs to the floor of the gymnasium. (Delaney was a carpenter when in prison). This had annoyed Gatzais to the point of threatening Delaney with his adze, a cutting tool with an arched blade which could have done some serious damage to Delaney had Gatzais really meant to use it. Up to now Robert Delaney had been behaving himself and his conduct had been described as 'fair'. He had only had 24 remission marks forfeited during the last twelve months. (These marks represented 3 days).

After being in Parkhurst for four years, *'prisoner No 474917 Delaney R,'* was assessed. At this time Robert was supposedly a Catholic and the chaplain reported that Robert had his own opinions on all subjects, but that it was difficult to get him to speak about his offences. He noted that the prisoner was very careless with regard to his religion, and although he had known Delaney for six months, all he could get him to promise was that he would 'make good' in South Africa. The chaplain remarked that Robert was intelligent and well educated and should have no difficulty in keeping out of prison, but that at the present time there was no evidence that he meant to lead an honest life.

The governor reported that Robert was fairly well behaved and worked reasonably hard in his role as a prison carpenter. He went on to say that Delaney should be able to earn an honest living when released but doubted that he had any intention of doing so. He also mentioned that Delaney had apparently lost touch with all his relatives.

This report gave Delaney's estimated date of release as 18th October 1933.

CHAPTER FIVE

1934

Delaney was released from gaol on licence in October 1933, and this time he managed to remain free for a year.

During this time Delaney pulled a few stunts, one of which backfired on him rather. He had broken into a house somewhere in London and was so engrossed in trying to open the safe that he didn't hear the butler entering the room until the light went on and a voice said 'Hello Delaney, so it's you!' This took him by surprise and threw him off balance until he realised the butler was someone he had known in gaol. The man was trying to go straight (which was more than Delaney was) and he was afraid that he would be suspected if Delaney got away with the jewels. He asked Delaney to do him a favour and not rob the safe this time for his sake. This would be to the advantage of them both he explained, as he would not lose his job when his employer found out he had a record, and Delaney wouldn't be in trouble because the police had been sent for. Delaney, who prided himself on being a gentleman, agreed and left empty handed.

One of the maddest things Delaney ever did, if we can believe him, was to break into a house and stay overnight. This was because the gates to the property were locked at midnight and were not opened again until 6am, so he had to get in before they were locked and remain until they were opened again. The house was a four storey mansion and Delaney got in through one of the top windows by his usual method of entry. It was an empty room and he sat down to wait for the return of the titled lady whose diamonds he was planning to steal. He smoked cigarette after cigarette trying to keep himself awake and at 2.30am he heard the limousine arriving. He waited for an hour to give the lady time to settle down and go to sleep and then he went along to her dressing room. Here he helped himself to her tiara, necklace and bracelet that she had carelessly left on her dressing table for her maid to put away the next day. He then went downstairs and read a book in the library until 6am when the gates would be reopened and he could leave! Delaney got £7000 for these jewels from his fence, but he was annoyed to learn from the newspapers that they were worth £30,000!

One night he had a narrow escape when, as he was coming down the stack pipe after having done the job, he fell giving himself quite a fright. It was a foggy night and the pipe was wet. His hands slipped and he fell through the air expecting disaster, but as he passed a window he managed to grab the sill and hang on. In doing so he had made quite a noise. He kept still and held his breath. The front door opened and then closed again. (He found out later that the maid had thought the thud he made when he fell was someone knocking at the door). When nothing else happened he struggled to reach the drainpipe again and managed to reach the floor in one piece. He made off just in time as the door opened again and a man came out walking off in a purposeful manner - to fetch the police, Delaney thought.

After a while Delaney decided that London was becoming 'too hot' for him and so he accepted an invitation to stay with some friends in Manchester. The first night, on going down to dinner, he was amazed at the amount of jewellery his hostess and her other house-guests were wearing. He decided then and there that this was his next job. The following day he went out shooting with the rest of the party, but all the while he was turning over in his mind various plans to steal the jewels. Whilst enjoying the day, Robert was not one to let an opportunity be lost. One of the young ladies accidentally threw her hat into a tree and it became lodged between two branches. She asked Robert to climb up and get it for her, but seeing an opportunity to establish an alibi he said he would have been delighted to do so, but couldn't climb a tree on account of an old war wound.

He decided to bide his time until Sunday when the routine of the house changed, and supper was served in the evening, instead of dinner. That meant that the ladies dressed a little less formally and would not be wearing their jewels. This would be his chance.

Pleading trouble with his fictitious 'war wound' Delaney retired to his room, explaining to his hostess that sleep was the only 'cure'. He waited until everyone had gone down to the dining room and then went along to his hostess's bedroom. He took her jewels, went back to his room and put them into his toilet bag, and then left the house in search of a suitable tree in which to hide the evidence. On his return to the house he entered by an upstairs window taking care to make it look as if a burglar had entered this way. He then returned to his bed and fell asleep. He was awakened at eleven o'clock by sounds of activity. The police had been sent for, but Delaney was not concerned, as he knew the local police would know nothing about him. There was no need to worry in any case, as when the detective was searching the house Robert's hostess would not let the policeman wake him, as she said her guest was not well and she did not want him disturbed!

Delaney stayed for a few more days and then returned to London, leaving the jewels hidden in the tree. He waited for two weeks before driving up one night to retrieve his cache. He sold the jewels for £5000 and used the money to go to Monte Carlo on a gambling spree.

Another time when trying to break into a shop, Delaney took a nasty fall and hurt his back and his legs. He made such a noise when falling that he had to lie quietly for ten minutes or so to see if anyone had heard him. When he realised no-one had, he got up and brushed himself down. He noticed a window leading into the cellar of the premises he had been trying to enter, so he took out his gadget for opening windows, and broke in through the cellar. He opened the safe and took out the money, left by the front door and hailed a taxi to take him home. As he always wore an evening suit when out doing a job nobody gave him a thought, as young men-about-town generally took a taxi home in the early hours of the morning. If he were limping from his fall it would have been assumed that he had been drinking! It took Delaney a week or two to recover from this fall. This episode must have made him realise that he was no longer as fit as he used to be, and may have been what led him to train young boys to do the climbing for him.

Eventually his luck must have run out as he appeared at West London Police Court on 13th November 1934. He was charged with breaking and entering a flat at the Royal Palace Hotel, Kensington on October 3rd and stealing jewellery to the value of £1,100 belonging to a Mrs Gluckstein. A further charge was brought against Delaney of inciting a teenage boy to break into a house at Kensington Palace Gardens on October 27th. He strongly denied this charge. Mr Melville, prosecuting, said that since the arrest it had come to the knowledge of the police that Delaney had begun to train a sixteen year old boy to become a burglar. He had taken him round to various houses and instructed him how to break in, and it had been the boy who had climbed up to the fifth floor flat at the Royal Palace Hotel and stolen the jewellery.

After his arrest this boy had visited Delaney in prison on at least four occasions. On one of these visits Delaney told the boy he wanted some money and gave him instructions how and where to get it. Having done the job he was to hide the stuff and then come again for further instructions as to the disposal of the loot. Unfortunately for Delaney the boy was arrested inside the house in Kensington Palace Gardens and was brought before the magistrates at the juvenile court. It seems that Delaney had met the boy a few months earlier and had set about training him to shin up drainpipes for nefarious purposes. This boy went by the name of 'Jackie', and had previously been working as a milkman.

Also appearing in court was Olive Delaney, aged 32, Robert's wife, who was charged with receiving some of the stolen goods. She was remanded on bail. Who was this woman? Had Delaney really married her? If so it was bigamously, for he had never divorced his wife Kitty.

A week later at a further hearing, another charge was brought against Delaney of breaking and entering a property in Bexhill-on-Sea. On October 19th he had broken into Sackville Lodge, Garry Hill, Bexhill, the home of Mr Enoch Horace Holmes. Despite the presence of a Scottish terrier, he had got away with jewellery, and other items including an automatic pistol.

Evidence was given by Mr Herbert Bond an apartment house keeper in Bexhill-on-Sea, that on October 10th a man and a woman accompanied by a boy called 'Jackie', took a room at his house for one week. They gave their names as Mr and Mrs James. Mr Bond identified Delaney as Mr James, and the boy, who was brought into the court, as the aforesaid 'Jackie'. Mr Bond said the three of them left his lodging house on October 17th and two days later he saw 'Jackie' take a train at Warrior Square Station for Polegate. Previously the same evening he had seen Delaney and the woman also waiting for a train to Polegate.

This boy, who was aged sixteen, then gave evidence to say that he met Delaney in a café in Leicester Square, where Delaney engaged him in conversation. They then went to Green Park, where Delaney questioned the boy as to his ability to climb. He asked the boy if he would like to earn some *'easy money'* and then took him home to meet Mrs Delaney who gave him some tea. Afterwards the Delaneys took the boy to the cinema.

The next day, following Mr Delaney's instructions, the boy said he climbed the fire escape at a hotel which had been previously pointed out to him. He entered by a window using a tool provided by Delaney, and stole the jewellery. He had been told they would meet afterwards at the library, but finding that Robert was not there, the boy showed some initiative and took a taxi back to the flat in Shaftsbury Avenue. Finding Delaney there, he handed the stolen goods to him and received ten shillings in payment. The next day Delaney gave him more money in the form of ten one pound notes.

Later he went to Bexhill-on-Sea with Mr and Mrs Delaney where they took lodgings, the boy passing as Mrs Delaney's younger brother. He said he was instructed to enter a house from which he stole some property, which included a cigarette case and some gold coins. This time he was told to meet Robert and Olive on the golf course. Mrs Delaney took the stolen goods from him, and they all went to the railway station to catch a train back to London.

After Delaney's arrest the boy visited him in Brixton gaol four times, during these visits Delaney told him about the house at Kensington Palace Gardens. He entered it to steal some property but was arrested in the act. Delaney had hoped to get money for his defence from the proceeds of this job. Delaney was remanded until the following Monday.

At his next appearance in court Robert Delaney was also charged with bigamy. He had married Olive Helen Louise Delaney, in July 1934. She was then a waitress but before that she had been on the stage. She was thirty two and nearer his age than his first wife had been. Olive had no previous convictions and the judge dealt leniently with her. He said that he was prepared to accept her story that she had acted under Delaney's influence, and when she married him she did not know that he was already married. She was bound over for two years.

Delaney was described by Inspector Lynch of New Scotland Yard as an extremely dangerous criminal. He said Delaney had for some time been strongly suspected of committing cat burglaries in London and the provinces, and it seemed that he had taken the boy in this case to the Green Park to show him buildings he wanted him to break into. He had even showed the boy photographs of himself entering windows.

Sir Percival Clarke when passing sentence on Delaney said he was quite satisfied that he was a menace to society. He said there was no doubt that he had used the services of a young man on the threshold of life in order to enrich himself and that, as Delaney was a convict on licence when the second offence was committed, the least possible sentence he could pass was one of nine years penal servitude!

CHAPTER SEVEN

The Later Years

Delaney must have been appalled to receive this sentence. It was the longest he had ever had, and his immediate response was to appeal. On the 5th February 1935 his petition was heard at the Court of Criminal Appeal, London, when his sentence was reduced by two years. However due to the fact that he was out on licence when he committed this crime, he had 714 days added on. This effectively wiped out the two years he had gained.

Delaney was sent to Dartmoor this time. In a petition dated 3rd December 1935 Delaney wrote to ask if he could be allowed to write and receive letters 'of a friendly nature' to Mr A G Carless, c/o Mutual Aid Society, 57 & 58 Chancery Lane, London WC2. He went on to say that if permission were denied he would like to know the reasons why. Mr Carless was an ex-prisoner and was supposedly the secretary of the Mutual Aid Society. The reply from the Under Secretary of State was short and to the point. It said that the petition dated 3rd December 1935 had been fully considered by the Secretary of State, but the request was denied. It was not possible to inform the prisoner of the reasons for this decision. What was Delaney up to now? A G Carless was at that time being investigated by the Director of Public prosecutions, and the authorities clearly thought he was not a suitable correspondent for Robert Delaney!

Robert Delaney seemed to have been behaving himself reasonably well whilst in prison, as we see in an assessment done four years later. In the report dated 17th December 1938, his expected release date was given as 30th August 1941. The medical officer reported that Delaney was in satisfactory general health and had rarely reported sick. He said the prisoner was quiet and reserved, and his mental condition was satisfactory. The chaplain also commented that Delaney was quiet, orderly and sensible. He was well read, conducted himself in a seemly manner and was quite candid concerning his past life, although he appeared to be unashamed of his conduct.

The Governor's Report was ominous: *'Works and behaves well – a model prisoner – will see the inside of many prisons before he ends his days.'*

However, in October 1940 the Home Office issued a statement to the effect that Delaney was to be released on licence the following month. So on 29th November 1940 Delaney was released on condition that should he be convicted again, the licence would be forfeited and another 1097 days would be added to any new convictions.

Sentenced again in 1941 for felony and receiving stolen goods, he was sent to Pentonville for three consecutive terms of three years. Delaney, who never did anything without a reason, now claimed to be a Unitarian and asked to be transferred to a prison with a Unitarian minister. Just what he had in mind we will never know, as he had previously been a Catholic, so he must have had some devious plan in mind. As requested he was moved to Parkhurst on the Isle of Wight.

Now Robert began a series of petitions to get his sentence reduced. He suggested that he should be released to help with the war effort. He wrote to the Secretary of State suggesting that he should have a reduction or cancellation of his sentence in order that he could fight for the country. He said he had served in France and Belgium in the last war, and up to the time of his arrest had been working at the War Office! This was all lies, as shortly after he had married Kitty Sharpe, Robert Delaney went absent without leave and was listed as a deserter. He also suggested that there was a dearth of skilled tradesmen and as he was highly skilled he felt he should put himself at their disposal. This did not have the desired effect and he was forced to write again at a later date and ask them to reconsider this petition.

The Secretary of State, however, was not to be swayed. Delaney was eventually informed that his petition had been considered, but he would have to complete much more of his term before he could expect an early release. Robert continued to petition the Secretary of State.

He then tried suggesting that his sentence should be shortened because the judge had said that he should have a considerably shorter term of imprisonment than his accomplice. The reason for this, Delaney said, was in order that they should not be released simultaneously and thus have the opportunity of joining up once more to pool their criminal tendencies. However, a letter from the Metropolitan Police stated that there were no records of the judge ever having said this. The notes of the official shorthand writer at the trial proved that all the judge suggested was that *'one good resolution to make today would be never to see each other again.'*

He was eventually released on the first of June 1945, but after only a few months of freedom he was appearing yet again before the magistrate, this time at Sussex Assizes in Lewes on 5th December of that same year. The charges were stealing £6,750 worth of jewellery from the home of Cyril Kleinwort of Haywards Heath on 8th September, receiving other jewellery worth £27, and breaking into a house at Sunninghill, Berkshire, where he stole nearly £2,000 worth of property. Also appearing in the dock were Leonard Reubens, aged 50, a jeweller of Hatton Gardens, and Mrs Catherine Trott, aged 65, of Harringay. Reubens was charged with receiving jewellery worth £5,660 and was sentenced to two years in prison; and Mrs Trott, who was charged with harbouring Delaney knowing him to have committed a felony received six months imprisonment. Delaney was convicted of housebreaking and larceny and given four years penal servitude.

Robert Delaney was now aged fifty and had spent much of his life behind bars. Would he never learn?

CHAPTER EIGHT

Conclusion

Delaney was now entering the last phase of his life. Sent to Parkhurst once more, it must have all seemed so familiar. Since the age of thirty he had spent more time in prison than out of it. Except for two short periods in 1933-34 and again in 1940-41 he had had very little freedom. He usually re-offended within months, if not weeks of his release, and was generally apprehended almost immediately. The police were probably watching him as soon as they knew he was free.

This was to be his last incarceration as his health was beginning to fail. He was nearing the end of his sentence, but had sixteen months left of a revoked licence to complete, when his niece, Miss Chere Allison, wrote to the Secretary of State at the Home Office on 6th October 1948 to plead his case. She said she was of the opinion that her uncle would *'make good'* if only he were allowed to return to South Africa. She said his relatives were willing to find him employment and that Delaney would pay all his travelling expenses! Where was he to find the money for these?

It had been said that he had lost touch with all his relatives in South Africa, but this could not have been the case. However Chere Allison's letter did not sway the Secretary of State. A note dated 19th October 1948 in the same file said that the Secretary of State had considered her letter but he could not release the prisoner Delaney any earlier than planned.

Even if Delaney had been released on compassionate grounds it would probably have been too late. Maybe he went into a decline knowing that he was not to be released as he had hoped, but less than a month later Delaney was dead. A note from the Governor to the Secretary of State said that the Commissioners had to report for the information of the Secretary of State, that the above-named Robert Delaney had died in Parkhurst Prison on the 14th December 1948.

An inquest was held the following day when the verdict returned was: 'Natural causes – Coronary Thrombosis due to Atheroma'.

A small item in the local newspaper said that an inquest had been held on Robert Delaney 53, a convict, of no fixed abode, who died on Tuesday. It went on to say that Delaney, who was born in South Africa, had completed three years of a four year sentence for housebreaking and larceny. Verdict was death from natural causes.

* * *

Robert Delaney had had a good start in life, if it was true that he had been well educated. However he told so many lies that we will never know just how he began. Efforts to trace his birth, both in South Africa and in Ireland have drawn a blank. It was impossible to trace any evidence of his having been educated by the Jesuits although he repeatedly tells the story of his schoolday escapades.

His stories of his army days too are all fiction as he deserted only a few months after arriving in this country. Did he desert to go and live with his new wife in Lincolnshire? Why was he not found and made to go back?

Having married a wealthy woman he could have applied himself to farming and tried to be a good husband, thus having a decent life. Instead he seems to have preferred to spend his time in more exciting pursuits and relished moments of risk. He was obviously fearless, as we saw in his account of his *'first job'*, when (if it were true) he took time to light a cigarette before walking down the stairs and out of his victim's front door.

He was quite heartless in his treatment of other people, both his victims and his accomplices. He was prepared to use a young boy and encourage him on a downward slide into crime when he took Jackie under his wing. And what had happened to Willie, his young brother of whom nothing more was ever heard? He married Olive without once considering the fact that he was still married to Kitty, and used her to the extent that she eventually had to do two years in prison. He must have used his charm to influence Leonard Reubens and Mrs Trott into helping him, both of whom were described by the judge as having the appearance of respectability. Neither of them had ever been in trouble with the police before. And of course there was Kitty, his wife, whose life he had completely ruined.

Kitty lived to be an old lady of ninety-two. In her later years her mind was affected by the turn her life had taken. In the late

A photograph (presumably posed for the paper) from Thompson's Weekly News, Saturday, September 15, 1934.

CERTIFIED COPY of an ENTRY OF DEATH
Pursuant to the Births and Deaths Registration Act 1953

HC 765471

Registration District **Isle of Wight**

1948. Death in the Sub-district of **Isle of Wight North** in the County of **Isle of Wight**

No.	When and where died	Name and surname	Sex	Age	Occupation	Cause of death	Signature, description, and residence of informant	When registered	Signature of registrar
140	Fourteenth December 1948 at The Hospital H.M. Convict Prison Parkhurst Newport I.O.W.	Robert DELANEY	Male	53 years	Foreman of Joinery:- of S. Africa (not known due to absence of details in this country) Carpenter & Joiner	Natural Causes :- Coronary Thrombosis	Certificate received from E F A Webster Coroner for the Isle of Wight Inquest held 15 Dec. 1948	Eighteenth December 1948	E M Cooper Deputy Registrar

Delaney's death certificate.

sixties when the 'meals on wheels' ladies arrived with her dinner they would be greeted by: 'What a terrible war this is', and she would talk about how lucky it was that we had Mr Churchill. She had become stuck in a time warp. She died in Pinchbeck Road Hospital, Spalding on the second of April, 1971. Cause of death was cerebral arteriosclerosis. On the death certificate she was described as being the widow of Robert Delaney!

When in prison Delaney had worked hard and was said to be a model prisoner. If he had only applied himself to honest work when he was free, he could have made a good living. He doesn't seem to have realised that he was now a known criminal and as such would be under observation when released on licence. He still seems to have thought that he could get away with his unlawful behaviour as he had done in the early days. 'Going straight' was never a consideration.

The governor who said that he would see the inside of many more prisons before he died, was correct in his assessment of Delaney's character. One of the chaplains in his report had also suggested that the prisoner did not seem sorry for what he had done, and whilst he recognised Robert's intelligence and potential for staying out of prison, he too thought it was most likely that he would re-offend.

Unfortunately Robert Delaney was so confident in his ability that he always thought he was clever enough to get away with it. He was inclined to blame ill luck when he was caught. It was never his fault!

REFERENCES

Newspaper cuttings

Boston Guardian
    24 January 1925
    07 February 1925
    14 February 1925
    05 November 1927
    12 November 1927
    08 December 1934
    15 December 1934
    22 December 1934

Boston Standard
    15 November 1927
    12 November 1927
    17 November 1934
    01 December 1934
    22 December 1934

The Times
    19 December 1945

Daily Sketch
    19 December 1945

News Chronicle
    19 December 1945

The Star
    19 December 1945

I.O.W. County Press
    18 December 1948

Thomson's Weekly News
    01 September 1934
    08 September 1934
    15 September 1934
    22 September 1934
    29 September 1934
    06 October 1934
    13 October 1934
    20 October 1934

Census entries

1851 census	**1881 census**	**1901 census**
HO107/2099/584	RG11/3220/5/9	RG13/3041/15
HO107/2099/664	RG11/3220/88/12	RG13/3040/8-9

Other items
Birth, Marriage and Death certificates.
Directories.
Records from the PRO: [from a folder marked HO45/22919]
Information found at the Essex Archives, Southend.
Various correspondence.